THE SCIENCE OF...
PROTECTING
THE PLANET

by
JEREMY SMITH
Consultant
MARTIN FISHER

ticktock
MEDIA

CONTENTS

Every day, things are happening on planet Earth that **threaten** wild plants and animals and the places in which they live. This has become such a serious problem that any people, in many countries, are working hard to try and save the natural world. The word '**conservation**' means the preservation or saving of the natural world - the **environment** - and especially of its plants, animals and other natural resources.

MANY AREAS

The main aim of a conservation scientist - also known as a **conservationist** - is to protect and save these plants, animals and **habitats** from damage, destruction and **extinction**. People who work full time as conservation scientists usually train in one of the disciplines of **biology**, such as **botany** (the study of plants), **zoology** (the study of animals), **marine biology** (the study of life in the sea) or **ecology** (the study of how the natural world works). They then use their knowledge to work towards the conservation of plants, animals, seas or habitats in

Monitoring the numbers and sizes of species help conservation scientists understand which animals are in danger.

One of the best known extinct creatures is the dodo. It was wiped out from its island home Mauritius by human hunters.

various parts of the world, and especially in those areas where the threats to their existence are greatest, such as the threat posed to the **rainforests** in the Amazon by logging. Since 1978 over half a million square kilometres of this forest has been destroyed.

PROTECTING SPECIES

Some conservation scientists may work with a particular **species** to ensure that it does not actually become extinct. Animal and plant breeding programs may provide special assistance, care and protection to allow young to be born, eggs to be hatched, seeds to germinate. Ongoing care helps the young to survive to maturity, and then to reproduce. If the species is no longer found living in the wild, scientists may try to find a suitable habitat and reintroduce it, helping it until it is safely established and able to survive independently.

COLLECTING DATA

The collection of information on changes in numbers of particular species of plants and animals over time is very important in conservation - this is known as long-term monitoring. People of all ages can take part in local and national monitoring schemes. People interested in conservation may also join one of the many national or international conservation organizations, such as the World Wide Fund for Nature (WWF). Money raised from the membership fees of these organizations goes towards conservation projects, and the Societies keep the members informed of current conservation problems and successes.

On the island of Surtsey, in Iceland, created by a volcano in 1963, conservationists were able to monitor the arrival of several species to the island.

Nothing in the natural world is constant. However, the needs of an increasing human population for food and space is having a huge effect on **habitats** and on their plant and animals. Every day, for example, thousands of acres of forest is cleared for farming and hundreds of **species** become **extinct**. **Conservation** is important because it aims to protect the natural world, to prevent species going extinct as a result of man's activities, and to prevent further habitat damage.

NATURAL THREATS

Some **threats** are natural and cannot be avoided. Droughts, floods and strong winds can damage large areas of land, affecting everything that lives there. Earthquakes and volcanoes, though rare, can also have devastating effects. An example was the eruption

Tiger researchers estimate that there are fewer than 2,500 tigers left in the world today.

of the Krakatoa volcano on the island of Rakata in the Pacific Ocean in 1883. The explosions were heard 2,200 miles away in Australia, and all life on the island was wiped out by a layer of sterile ash.

SCIENCE CONCEPTS

CONDITIONS FOR LIFE

All living things have some basic requirements in order to survive. They need a habitat to which they are suited (in the case of the polar bears shown right, the Arctic), with an adequate food supply. They must be safe from **predators** or anything else that could harm them, and be able to reproduce successfully. If all of these are present, they will survive. If any is missing, survival is unlikely – for example, stag beetle numbers have declined rapidly as its natural habitat of dead wood has been cleared.

Many people think that pollution from smelly factories and people's houses has caused the temperature on Earth to rise. A rise in temperature will erase many habitats.

Since that time biologists have been monitoring the recolonization of the island by plants and animals.

MAN-MADE THREATS

More serious long-term threats are the result of man's activities. The clearance of land for farming, building and roads, and by logging, destroys natural habitats. This is a very serious problem. Fragmentation of natural habitats is also a major problem. One of the effects of land clearance is that natural habitats are broken up into smaller and smaller patches or fragments. Large carnivores such as tigers require very large areas of forest to hunt for their food. If these areas are too smaller they cannot survive, or they may survive by hunting on farmland, which brings them into conflict with people and their livestock.

CHANGING OUR WAYS

Conservation organizations not only work to establish protected areas and save species, they also work to persuade governments to bring in new laws to protect habitats and individual species. Another important part of their work is to persuade major industries such as logging and oil companies to modify the way they carry out their work, so as to reduce or eliminate harmful effects to the **environment**. Conservation organizations are also starting to work in partnership with people to help them manage their local natural resources.

✎ SCIENCE SNAPSHOT

Some data indicates that the climates on Earth are getting warmer – a process called 'global warming' - which scientists think is due to pollution of the atmosphere. As the Earth warms up, many habitats will change or be destroyed. Unless they are able to adapt to these habitat changes, animals will have to migrate to new areas.

The fate of the saiga antelope has fluctuated over the years, and is now critical.

Before **conservation** scientists can begin to carry out any conservation work, they need to know which **habitats** or living things are **threatened** with **extinction**, and what those threats are. Because changes in the natural world often take place slowly, **conservationists** try to monitor changes in **habitats** and their **species** over several years. They then look for patterns in the data for clues about the risks that specific living things are facing or may face in the future.

ASSESSING THE THREAT

In order to assess the risk of extinction, and to be able to compare risks of extinction around the world, a standardized system is used. Conservationists have designed a set of categories, known as the Red List

CATEGORY	DESCRIPTION	EXAMPLE
Critically Endangered	Extremely high risk of extinction	Leatherback turtle, giant ibis
Endangered	Very high risk of extinction in the wild	Swan goose and giant panda
Vulnerable	High risk of extinction in the wild	Cheetah, Himalayan black bear
Near Threatened	Could become threatened in the future	Green salamander
Extinct in the Wild	Only survives in botanic gardens or zoos	Red-tailed shark, Saharan oryx
Extinct	Does not survive anywhere	Martinique parrot, Falklands wolf

The Red List is published every year and details the state of all of Earth's threatened species.

categories, to assess the risk of extinction (Red being for danger). The International Union for the Conservation of Nature (IUCN), based in Geneva, Switzerland, maintains the international Red List. The Red List started in the 1980s and new editions are now published each year on the internet. The Red List gives information about all species known to be at risk of extinction, including which of the Red List categories they fall into.

CHANGING THREATS

Because nature is not static, the figures change from one year to the next. Some species may, for example, become more threatened and will be moved to a more serious category of threat (e.g. from **Endangered** to **Critically** Endangered). A good example of this is the

SCIENCE CONCEPTS

SURVEYS

For surveys such as those carried out for the Red List (right) be valid and useful, they have to be carried out scientifically. Observations and records must be precise and accurate. Everything about the survey must be kept exactly the same every time observations are repeated, so that the only thing that changes is the number of individuals counted. It is rather like carrying out a 'fair test' in an investigation – you choose one variable that will change and keep everything else the same.

In some cases scientists are dispatched to a threatened habitat immediately to carry out surveys.

saiga, a **nomadic** antelope that lives in Central Asia. It has been hunted for many years for its meat and for the horns of the males, which are used in traditional Chinese medicine. From about one million animals in 1980 the saiga had declined to about 180,000 in 2000. At this time the saiga was categorized as Near Threatened on the Red List, but following further declines, its risk of extinction was upgraded to Critically Endangered in 2002. Species that are the subject of **conservation** action may be moved to a less threatened category, or be removed from the Red List altogether.

LOOKING FROM SPACE

Conservationists look over a satellite map of grizzly bear habitat in the Alberta foothills and Rocky Mountains.

Satellites can be used to gather information.
Looking at the surface of Earth from space, they can monitor migration patterns, and locate breeding grounds and winter homes. Whole habitats and **environmental** conditions can be monitored in this way. This is an exciting development in conservation science and one which is set to expand in the future.

SCIENCE SNAPSHOT

If a major wildlife threat is imminent, Conservation International, a worldwide organisation, sends out rapid assessment teams (RAPs), made up of expert international field biologists, to a specific area. They stay for three or four weeks and gather as much information as they can about the habitat and its wildlife. They then pass on the information, so that the danger can be averted. This system has helped to set up national parks in Bolivia and Peru, saving habitats that would otherwise have been destroyed.

One problem that **conservation** organizations, governments and **conservationist** scientists always face is that the money required for the establishment of protected areas or other forms of conservation is always in short supply. This means that not all sites that require protection can be protected. Conservationists therefore have to decide which are the areas that require protection most urgently.

The island of Soqotra contains unique species of plants and is of particular value to conservationists.

BIODIVERSITY AND ENDEMISM

Biodiversity refers to the number of types, or species, of plants and animals in a particular place. Areas that are particularly rich in biodiversity - such as

the **tropical** forests of the Amazon and of South-east Asia - are of particular conservation importance and may require special protection. **Endemism** refers to — that are found only within a particular restricted place, such as in a particular mountain range, or a particular country. For example, the island of Soqotra in the Indian ocean has a high diversity of plant species, and 35% of these are found only on this island and nowhere else in the world.

ECOREGIONS

The conservation organization WWF has created a conservation strategy based on a concept known as **Ecoregions**. An Ecoregion is an area of land or water that contains a distinct grouping of plants and animals. The Conservation Science Program of WWF has identified a very large number of Ecoregions around

SCIENCE CONCEPTS

IDENTIFYING SPECIES

To be able to conserve organisms such as the leatherback turtle (right) it is vital to be able to identify the species that are threatened. Every distinct species has two Latin names; the first is the genus, and the second is the species. For example, the tiger is *Panthera tigris*. Tigers from different areas may be slightly different in appearance and then a third name, a subspecies is used. For example, the Siberian tiger is *Panthera tigris altaica*, and the Bengal tiger of India is *Panthera tigris tigris*.

Areas such as the Arctic and the creatures that live there are especially sensitive to change. Zoologists here are taking samples from tranquilized polar bears to see if these bears have been affected by pesticides used in the area.

the world - about 850 - and amongst these it has identified the 200 most biologically distinct terrestrial, freshwater, and marine ecoregions of the planet, and these are the areas in which the organization is concentrating its conservation efforts.

New species of animals such as this deep sea shrimp are being found every year by conservationists.

HOTSPOTS

The conservation organization Conservation International has created a conservation strategy based on what are known as **Hotspots**. A Hotspot is an area of the world that has been reduced to less than 10% of its original vegetation and that contains the most **threatened** reservoirs of plant and animal life on Earth. This strategy is based both on biodiversity and on the degree of threat (i.e. the Red List status). The world's 25 most important global Hotspots are one of Conservation International's main areas of focus for biodiversity conservation. An example of a hotspot is the Western Ghats mountain range and tropical forest in south-west India.

SCIENCE SNAPSHOT

Nobody knows exactly how many species of plants, animals, fungi and other organisms have so far been discovered and named, but it's probably about 1 million. It has been estimated, however, that there are possibly about 10 million species on the Earth, and most of the undiscovered species are in the wet tropical forests. Many of these undiscovered and unnamed species are insects, which are very diverse in tropical forests.

PROTECTED AREAS

One of the main ways that **conservationists** seek to protect the natural world is by the establishment of protected areas. These are areas in which all of the **organisms** in an area - whether the **habitat** is desert, woodland, wetland, or a coral reef in the sea - are protected from hunting, **deforestation** and other damage.

TYPES OF PROTECTED AREA

Protected areas can be large or small, and can have different forms of protection. The IUCN has created a system for categorizing protected areas. There are seven different types of protected area, from a Strict Nature Reserve (managed for scientific study or protection of its wilderness) to a Managed Resource Protected Area, managed for the **sustainable** use of its natural resources.

HOW ARE IMPORTANT AREAS PROTECTED?

The first step in setting up a protected area is usually for it to be protected

This satellite photo shows the protected Galapagos Islands as seen from space.

by the law of the country concerned. After that, it is usual to employ rangers or guards to look after the area. The rangers carry out regular patrols of the protected area to prevent any poaching, for example, and they may also be involved in monitoring of the wildlife. Monitoring means that they carry out regular **surveys** or counts of particular **species**, to know whether there is a healthy number of individuals. In some protected areas where there is heavy poaching (such as for elephant tusks for ivory in some areas of East Africa), the guards have to be armed for their own protection.

SCIENCE CONCEPTS

SCIENCE OR TOURISM?

Many people have different views as to exactly what should be preserved in a protected area. Some people think it is most important to protect the scenery, particularly as that is what the general public are most interested in. The beauty of protected areas brings tourism and with it money. On the other hand, many conservationists argue that the entire ecosystem is what matters most, including the smaller, less attractive **species**, such as the grasses and insects present there, and that just looking after the more dramatic elements of an area creates a false facade rather than a scientifically valuable natural area.

Conservationists trying to protect the scarlet macaw have faced confrontations with armed poachers.

HOW MUCH OF PLANET EARTH IS PROTECTED?

More and more areas of the earth and sea are being protected from damage. At the end of 2003 about 11.5% of the land area of the earth received some sort of protection, but less than 0.5% of the seas of the world are protected. The two largest protected areas on the land are the North-East Greenland IUCN Category II National Park of Greenland with an area of 9,720 km2, and the 6,400 km2 Ar'Rub al Khali Category VI Wildlife Management Area of Saudi Arabia. The two largest marine protected areas are the Great Barrier Reef Category VI Marine Park of Australia covering 3,444 km2, and the 3,412 km2 Northwestern Hawaiian Islands Category VI Coral Reef Ecosystem Reserve.

A ranger of the Kenyan Wildlife Service holds an elephant tusk confiscated from poachers.

SCIENCE SNAPSHOT

Sometimes protecting **endangered** species and **habitats** can be very dangerous. In Guatemala, the scarlet macaw has become endangered because its chicks are being caught and sold for exotic pets for hundreds of dollars. Poachers have been following scientists sent to Guatemala to **survey** the chicks in order to find the nests. Once the scientists have finished surveying bird numbers, they are confronted and forced to flee the area. To counter the threat the government has given research scientists armed guards whenever they are sent out into the forest.

In the past, many zoos simply kept animals in cages and people paid to go and see them. In recent years, however, there have been major changes in zoos. Keepers now try hard to recreate conditions found in the animals' natural **habitats**, giving them more space and keeping them in groups rather than caged individually. Both zoos and **botanic** gardens now also have new roles to play, as a place for the breeding of **threatened** animals and plants.

Snow leopards are bred in captivity to ensure the survival of the species.

SAVING SPECIES

Both zoos and botanic gardens now also have new roles to play, as places for the breeding of threatened animals and plants. Although conditions in a zoological or botanic garden can never be exactly the same as in the wild, these gardens do provide some benefits. Zoological gardens can help to ensure the survival of threatened **species** by providing them with a secure environment in which they can breed. Botanic Gardens can provide a similar advantage for plants by providing the right soil and water conditions.

A HELPING HAND

Breeding programmes can help to increase the numbers of individuals of a threatened species. A well-known example of this is the success of zoos around the world in rearing giant panda cubs. Another well-known example is that of the Arabian oryx. The last few wild individuals of the oryx were captured in order to prevent them from being hunted. They bred very successfully in captivity, and have now been reintroduced into the wild in several countries. From only a handful of individuals there are now a total of

SCIENCE CONCEPTS

REPRODUCTION

Survival of a species depends on the balance between birth rates and death rates. For a population to remain stable, young must be born at the same rate as others die. If the birth rate is higher than the death rate, as is the case with animals like rabbits and pigs (right), the population will expand and flourish. If the birth rate is lower than the death rate, as is the case with pandas, the population will shrink and eventually become **endangered**.

Many people feel uneasy about the thought of wild animals being kept behind bars in zoos, but zoos also help to prevent endangered species from becoming totally extinct.

Giant pandas are so rare that zoos play a crucial role in the preserving the species.

about 4,000 oryx, reintroduced into the wild and in zoos, worldwide.

PAYING THEIR WAY

Maintaining a zoo, looking after the animals in it and running breeding programmes is very expensive, so zoos need to raise money. Most do this by charging the public an entry fee to see the animals. Some also run animal adoption schemes, where people pay some money towards the maintenance of an individual bird or animal. Some zoos have government funding and some may be registered as charities.

Rare birds such as this spectacular red kite have been released back into the wild after successful zoo breeding programmes.

SCIENCE SNAPSHOT

Many people approve of zoos, seeing nothing in wrong keeping animals in captivity. Many other people think that we have absolutely no right to do this. Arguments go backwards and forwards, as people try to balance animal rights and suggestions about captivity being cruel against the benefits of regular feeding, safety from predators, veterinary care and breeding programmes.

All animals and plants **evolve** in a particular place and then spread naturally. With the speed of modern transport, such as cars and boats, some species are being carried around the world and introduced into countries where they are not naturally found. A type of plant or animal introduced, either deliberately or accidentally, into a country of which it is not **native** is known as an alien **species**.

WHAT IS AN INVASIVE SPECIES?

In many cases the introduction of an alien species has little effect on the **habitat** in which it is introduced. However, some species, especially those that are able to reproduce quickly and in large numbers, become invasive, and are then known as invasive alien species. As an example, the small Indian mongoose, which eats other small animals, was introduced onto the sugar cane plantations of the Pacific Island of Fiji with the aim that it would eat the rats that were plaguing the sugar cane crop. However, the mongoose found that the native Fijian lizards and frogs were easier to catch, and they mostly ignored the rats.

The introduction of the small Indian mongoose to Fiji backfired when it started to prey on lizards and frogs rather than the rats it was brought in to catch.

NEW PROBLEMS

In the case of the Indian mongoose introduced into Fiji, several of the lizards and frogs that lived on the ground, rather than in trees, and were therefore easy to catch, were driven to **extinction** on several Fijian islands. Plants species that are very hardy and produce a lot of seeds can also, in the wrong place, become invasive aliens. Other types of **organism** can also be invasive. For example, in the early part of the 20th century a fungal disease known as chestnut **blight** was introduced by accident from Asia into North America and nearly drove the American Chestnut Tree to extinction by the fungus.

SCIENCE CONCEPTS

THE SPREAD OF ALIEN SPECIES

Organisms can be carried around the world in the holds of ships, stuck inside the tread of car trees, in crops such as bananas that are shipped from country to country, and by many other means. For example, when ships move heavy cargo around the world, they need to take water as ballast for the return journey. A ship may take in ballast water in the Indian Ocean and then sail to the Atlantic Ocean. Before they can reload with cargo they have to empty their ballast water. This ballast water may contain alien marine species from the Indian Ocean. In addition, some species have also been introduced deliberately to another habitat and country, often misguidedly.

The barnacle-like zebra mussel poses a multi-billion dollar threat to North America.

The Spectacled Caiman has been introduced into the United States from Central and South America. It now competes with native alligators for food.

COMBATING THE ALIENS

The best way of stopping foreign species settling is to stop them being brought into the country in the first place. Across the world, new laws have been put in place which make boat owners clean their boats thoroughly every time they travel. **Ballast** water exchange programmes have also been set up to try to ensure water from arriving boats are not dumped into foreign shores. If a species does manage to establish itself in a new country, then **conservationists** need to act to wipe them out as quickly as possible. Conservationists in the United States are particularly worried about the Asian longhorned beetle settling in the country, and have set up a hotline for anyone who spots one of these creatures so that they can be destroyed as quickly as possible. In Maryland in 2002 state authorities drained a lake to kill off the longhorned beetle after a sighting from a member of the public.

⚡ SCIENCE SNAPSHOT

Over the last one hundred years, over 4,500 foreign plants and animals have established themselves in the United States. The cost of invasive species to the US economy is a massive $137 billion per year. Invasive species have also hurt the country's endangered native species, causing these species to decline by nearly 50%. Invasive species also **threaten** nearly two thirds of the habitats of America's endangered species. An incredible three million acres of habitat are lost every year as a result.

As a result of the successful **conservation** breeding in zoos of animals that are either extinct in the wild or reduced to very low numbers, there have been sufficient numbers of some **species** to allow **reintroduction** into the wild. Reintroduction normally happens within some type of protected area, so that the reintroduced animals can be protected and will have a high chance of survival. One of the most important aims of reintroduction is that the reintroduced animals will breed and produce wild-born offspring.

Around 100,000 Yellowstone Park visitors have watched the wolves since their return in 1995.

THE ARABIAN ORYX

One of the best known and successful reintroductions was that of the white or Arabian oryx to several Arabian countries. In 1964 Operation Oryx captured the last few known wild oryx in southern Arabia on the border of Yemen and Oman. To these individuals were added a few more that were already in private zoos. This group, which became known as the World Herd, was moved to Phoenix Zoo in the US, where they bred very successfully. In 1980 individuals were returned to Oman, in Arabia, and released into an unfenced protected area. Oryx were able to roam freely in the wild once more. At a later date oryx were also released into two protected areas in Saudi Arabia, one unfenced and one fenced.

WOLVES IN YELLOWSTONE NATIONAL PARK

In the USA, Northern Rocky Mountain wolves were native to Yellowstone National Park when it was established in 1872. However, predator control was practised here in the late 1800s and early 1900s and by the 1970s, there was

SCIENCE CONCEPTS

REINTRODUCTION PROBLEMS

When an animal has gone **extinct** in the wild there are usually only a few animals in captivity from which to breed individuals for reintroduction. For example, the global population of about 4,000 oryx (shown left) are descended from only eight individuals, which means that there are only eight types of genetic variation in the global oryx gene pool. When conservationists reintroduce oryx into a new protected area they therefore try to ensure that all of the eight original types of variation are present amongst the reintroduced animals.

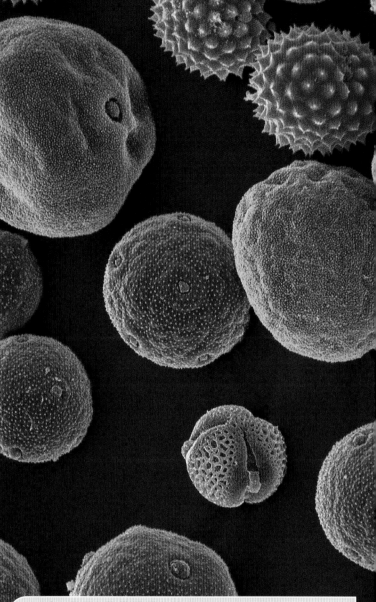

These pollen grains are amplified many thousands of times under a scanning electron microscope.

no wolf population in Yellowstone. In the 1990s a plan was developed to capture wolves in Canada and to reintroduce them to Yellowstone. In 1995, 14 wolves were released into and in 1996, 17 more wolves were brought from Canada and released. The first 14 wolves bore 2 litters totalling nine pups. In 1996, four packs produced 14 pups. The return of the only species known to be missing from the world's first National Park for the past half-century has been a milestone in reintroduction.

A CONTINUING SUCCESS STORY

To date, 19 species have been reintroduced into the wild after being bred in captivity. In the case of the Pere David's deer, Arabian Oryx, American bison, Red wolf, Guam kingfisher, Guam rail, and the California condor, the animal was extinct in the wild when the programme began. Other species including the bald eagle and the alpine ibex have put back into the wild in places where they used to live. In the case of the bald eagle, the bird can now been seen flying in the skies over Catalina Island for the first time in decades.

In 1987 the last few wild California condors were captured and put into a breeding programme at the Los Angeles Zoo and the San Diego Wild Animal Park.

SCIENCE SNAPSHOT

T he Millenium Seed Bank Project is a global conservation project at Kew Gardens in London. Botanists there aim to collect and conserve seeds from thousands of plant species from all over the world. They also want to research and improve seed conservation, to provide seeds for botanical research and to be able to reintroduce species back into the wild. This should ensure the survival of many plant species that might otherwise become extinct.

People are much more aware of **environmental** and **conservation** issues than they were in the past and many try hard to protect and conserve the living things around them. Scientists are constantly discovering new **species** and developing better ways of looking after the natural world.

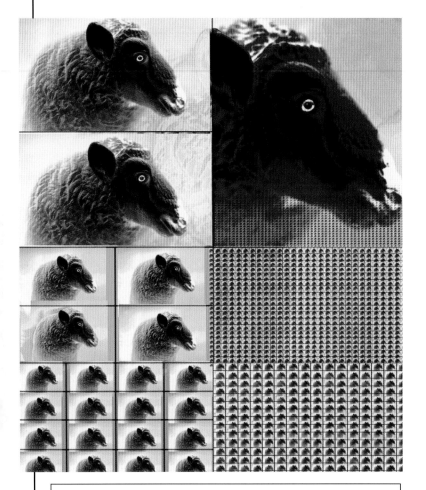

The possibilities of cloning may prove a way to save endangered species in the near future.

USING TECHNOLOGY

Some of the most exciting developments in conservation science are in the area of **genetics** — the study of inheritance. Geneticists have developed ways of taking a cell from an individual and '**cloning**' it to produce a new, genetically-identical individual. This could be very important in saving an **endangered** species from **extinction**, as it provides a way of increasing the numbers. Modern technology, developed for other purposes, can often help conservation efforts. For example, **satellite** tagging can be used to track individual animals. In New Zealand, tiny **transmitters** have been attached to dolphins' fins. These send out signals that are detected by satellites, which then send information about the dolphins' location back to scientists on Earth. However, not all **conservationists** approve — some say implanting the transmitter causes the dolphins more stress than the information is worth.

SCIENCE CONCEPTS

ECONOMY VS HABITAT

All over the world, habitats are being destroyed, often because of money. Rainforests and other natural habitats contain valuable materials that, in a poor country, can be sold to create wealth. A lot of international co-operation and financial support will be necessary if this is to stop. In richer countries, habitats are destroyed as societies expand. Pollution is also another major issue – it is easy to create rubbish but expensive to dispose of it in an environmentally-friendly way. Governments will need to decide how to balance the needs of the people with the needs of the natural world.

Planting your garden with flowers that bloom and produce nectar in the fall can attract an array of beautiful butterflies.

Two conservationists look at reseeded grazing lands over a disused open-pit mine in the United States.

LEARNING FROM THE PAST

Some governments have begun to realise the damage that people have done to the natural world in the past. By working together, and listening to advice from conservation scientists, these governments are trying to find ways of ensuring that such mistakes are not repeated. In many countries, natural **habitats** have been destroyed as people have built roads, towns and large industrial sites. At the same time, old buildings in city centres are often demolished. Increasingly, people are being encouraged to rebuild on the sites of old buildings (brownfield sites) instead of using up any more countryside (greenfield sites).

CHANGING THE LAW

Some laws may be necessary to prevent environmental damage — if there are severe penalties for breaking these laws, people may be less likely to do so. In other cases, education may help — if people know about the effects their actions may have on the natural world, and understand about conservation issues, they may choose to live their lives in a more environmentally friendly way.

SCIENCE SNAPSHOT

Everybody can play a part on conserving nature. There are groups all over the world, so there is probably one close to you that you could join. Some projects are global, but some are small and local – you could put up a bat box in your garden, for example, or plant some insect-friendly flowers. There may be local groups that need help clearing out ponds or stream. You could also take part in a national survey by watching the wildlife in your own garden.

Whales are amazing creatures. Although they live in water, they are mammals. This means that they have lungs and breathe air. They are warm-blooded and have live babies that suckle milk from their mothers. Aerial **surveys, satellite** tracking, photoidentification and deepwater videoprobes are all being used by **marine biologists** to gather data about whales.

The number of whaling ships has fallen in recent years.

CONTINUED THREAT

Between 1904 and 1967, more than 350,000 Blue Whales were killed in the Southern Hemisphere. In 1967, they were given legal protection, but not all countries agreed with this and some continued whaling. Blue Whales continue to need protection. Hardly any are caught by whalers now, but man is not the only **threat** to them. They rely on **plankton** for their food, and many marine biologists think that, if climate changes continue, this may become scarce. The lack of food would mean that many Blue Whales would not survive. Several international organisations have been set up to protect and conserve whales, and to let people everywhere find out more information about them.

RESCUE RESPONSE

Every year, many whales swim too close to the shore and become stranded. In Scotland, a special Whale and Dolphin Ambulance is now in use. This is a Land Rover, specially adapted to carry veterinary supplies and vital equipment to enable rescuers to locate, treat and re-float stranded whales. Many whales also die after colliding with ships or becoming tangled in fishing gear. A trial scheme is being set up off the coast of the USA to try to reduce these accidents. Buoys are being fitted with hydrophones (instruments that detect underwater sounds), **transmitters** and other electronic equipment. These will detect right whale sounds, and transmit information about the location of the whales to the ships' captains. The vessels can then be manoeuvred to avoid the whales.

Some people from traditional whaling communities argue it is their right to continue to hunt whales.

- *There are two groups of whales: toothed and baleen*
- *Blue Whales are the largest creatures ever to have lived on Earth*
- *If whales swim too close to the shore they may be stranded on the beach.*
- *In some places, the Blue Whale populations are now growing in size*
- *Climate change may mean many Blue Whales will die from lack of food.*

Whales are among the largest group of animals to have ever existed.

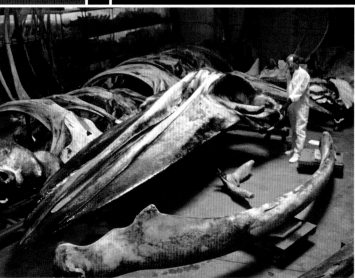

Whales have traditionally been caught not just for their blubber but also for their bones, which were used as tools and building materials.

Gorillas are the largest of the great apes and they can live to be around fifty years old. Gorillas share many of the characteristics of humans – in fact, the name gorilla means 'hairy person'. They use their faces to convey emotions, and, just like humans, their faces are different from one another. This means that **zoologists** can easily identify and monitor individuals.

A PEACEFUL SPECIES

There are two **species** of gorilla, each of which can be divided into two smaller groups, and they are all **endangered**. The Eastern gorillas are the Mountain gorillas and the Grauer's gorillas. The Western gorillas are the Western lowland gorillas and the Cross River gorillas. Mountain gorillas, also called 'Cloud gorillas' because they live high up in mountain forests, are the most at risk, and are on the verge of becoming **extinct**. They are found only in a small area in central Africa, on the Virunga volcanic mountains, which span the countries of Uganda, Rwanda and the Democratic Republic of Congo.

MANY THREATS

There are several main **threats** to gorillas. Their **habitat** is shrinking as people clear it for agriculture and logging. Fighting and wars have also destroyed much of their habitat. Gorillas are hunted and poached, being killed for the 'bushmeat' trade. There are no mountain gorillas held in captivity in any legal zoo or private collection anywhere in the world, but some adult female gorillas are killed and their babies taken to be sold as illegally as pets.

Gorillas have distinctive faces, just like humans, and act like humans sometimes, too.

Logging has destroyed many of the mountain gorillas habitats.

RESCUE EFFORT

Some groups of people are working hard to save the Mountain gorillas. The Virunga National Park offers some **habitat** protection and safety from poachers. The International Gorilla **Conservation** Programme (IGCP) has set up a ranger-based monitoring system to collect data and target specific help in areas where it is most needed. However, fierce fighting in the areas in which the gorillas live has disrupted the work of the **conservationists** as many rangers and park wardens have been in danger and unable to continue their work. The maps of the area of the Virunga National Park are very old and out of date. This has made it difficult to monitor the gorillas accurately. New geo-information systems using **satellites** is being used to produce up-to-date maps of the land and the vegetation. Also, with these geo-information systems, scientists can predict future changes and outcomes, which will help them to plan effective long-term strategies for helping the gorillas.

CASE STUDY FACTFILE

- *All gorillas are endangered*
- *The male gorilla is twice the size of the female*
- *The gorilla's only enemies are leopards and humans. Crocodiles can be dangerous to lowland gorillas.*
- *Habitat destruction is a big threat because the rich volcanic soil there is valued highly as farming land.*
- *Mountain gorillas do not reproduce very quickly. Females give birth for the first time at about age 10 and will have more offspring every three or four years.*

GORILLA DISTRIBUTION

Western Lowland Gorilla

Mountain Gorilla

Eastern Lowland Gorilla

Today, gorillas are restricted to a just a few areas in Africa.

The Golden Sun Moth used to be widespread in Australasian grasslands, living among wallaby grass and spear grass. Today, only about one per cent of this grassland remains. Some has been destroyed by spreading towns. Agriculture has also destroyed much, with wetland drainage, tree planting, overgrazing and use of **pesticides** and fertilisers. The Golden Sun Moths are now restricted to a few small, isolated sites.

LIFE CYCLE OF THE MOTH

Entomologists studying the Golden Sun Moth do not know full details about its life cycle, but they think it probably takes 2-3 years. Female sun moths lay eggs singly between plants and the soil. After hatching, the **larvae** tunnel into the plant, feeding on the plant tissue. The larvae then build short, silk-lined tunnels into the soil to feed on roots. Each makes a **pupa**, from which the adult moth emerges. The adults only survive for about two days, unable to feed because they do not have mouthparts. In this short time, eggs are laid ready to start the next generation. If anything happens to the adults during their short life, eggs are not laid and there can be no next generation.

HABITAT MANAGEMENT

The Golden Sun Moth is critically **endangered**, but many people are working to ensure its survival. **Surveys** have been carried out to identify sites where colonies survive. **Habitat** management plans have

The adult Golden Sun moth lives for just two days.

been put into action to ensure that the areas of grassland suitable for the moths expand. Because pesticides kill the moths, farmers have been asked to avoid using pesticides at the times when the adult moths are flying and laying eggs. The female moths cannot fly very far, so are unable to move from one site to another. Grassland areas are being planted to try to link isolated sites together, enabling the moths to breed more easily.

CAPTIVE BREEDING

Another main line of work involves captive breeding of moth populations. This increases the number of moths so that some can be reintroduced to suitable natural habitats. It also allows entomologists to study the moths very closely, in the hope that this will help them to understand the moth populations more fully. By looking at the genetic material of the moths, scientists can learn about how the moth populations have spread and separated. Scientists also hope that, by studying the Golden Sun Moth, they will develop a greater understanding of other insect populations and the **threats** that they face.

This scientist is extracting a sample of body fluid from a moth larva for genetic analysis.

CASE STUDY FACTFILE

- *The Golden Sun Moth is found in the grasslands of Australasia*
- *They are now only survive in a few isolated sites*
- *Native grassland once covered millions of hectares across southern Australia*
- *Around 1,500 Golden Sun moths still survive at the York Park Conservation Site*
- *The Golden Sun Moth has been collected by entomologists for more than 100 years and is one of the most studied insects of ecological interest in Australia.*

The Golden Sun Moth is found only in a small area of grassland in southeastern Australia.

Rainforests are found in hot, damp lands around the equator known as the '**equatorial belt**'. These areas have at least 4,000 mm of rain every year, with no dry season, and an average daily temperature between 21°C and 27°C. More than half of the world's estimated 10 million **species** of plants, animals and insects live in the tropical rainforests. Despite this, vast areas of rainforests are destroyed every year. In less than 50 years, more than half of the world's tropical rainforests have been destroyed and the rate of destruction is still accelerating.

A CRUCIAL RESOURCE

Rainforests are important for many reasons. They are often referred to as 'the lungs of the world', because of the amount of carbon dioxide the plants use up and the oxygen they put back into the air. Destroying rainforest affects everything that lives there. Trees and other plants die. Animals cannot survive without their shelter and food sources. Native peoples that have lived in the rainforests for thousands of years lose their homes and their natural ways of life. Some rainforest plants have been found to provide important medicines and foods. Many of the native peoples are very knowledgeable about their lands and can guide scientists towards new discoveries in these areas. However, as the rainforests are destroyed, much of this knowledge is lost forever.

TRAIL OF DESTRUCTION

Trees are cut down for their wood, such as mahogany, which is valuable. The process of harvesting the wood destroys everything else around it too, as **habitats** vanish, soil is lost due to **erosion** and air and water are polluted.

Rainforests provide homes for many rare species, including the orang-utan.

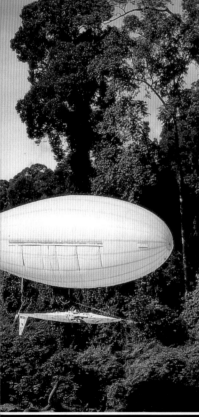

At least half of all the animal and plant species in the world live in rainforests.

Some researchers float over the forest in airships to carry out their research.

Lush, fertile lands are left bare and barren. If an area of rainforest is destroyed before scientists have had a chance to study it carefully, we may lose species that we never even knew existed.

RESCUE EFFORTS

Conservationists are trying hard to save the rainforests. Providing information to people about the consequences of what is happening to the rainforests is helping to reduce the demand for hardwoods. Financial assistance from other countries can help to set up alternative, sustainable projects in countries where logging was economically important, while some drug companies are investing in the rainforests in the hope that new drugs can be potentially made from the tropical plants that grow there.

CASE STUDY FACTFILE

- *Rainforests once covered around 14% of the earth's land surface. Today they cover just 6% and if the current rate of destruction continues they will totally disappear within 40 years.*
- *Experts estimates that we are losing 137 plant, animal and insect species every single day due to rainforest deforestation.*
- *Rainforest plants have been used in traditional medicines for hundreds of years*
- *Economic assistance from rich countries can help to save rainforest areas*
- *500 years ago there were around 10 million Indians living in the Amazonian Rainforest. Now there are less than 200,000.*

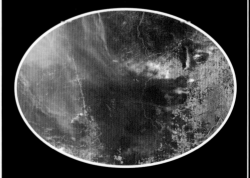

This satellite picture shows a section of the Amazon rainforest. The light regions show areas of deforestation.

ballast material put in the hold of a ship to enhance stability.

blight plant disease resulting in sudden wilting and dying of the affected parts

biology science of life and living organisms

biodiversity term for the number and variety of organisms found within a specified geographic region

botanist person who studies plants

clone process whereby a genetically-identical individual can be recreated from the information inside a cell

conservation The protection, preservation, management, or restoration of wildlife and of natural resourcesuch as forests, soil, and water.

conservationist a scientist who specialises in conservation

critical in conservation, an organism which is in imminent danger of extinction

deforestation the removal of trees

ecology science of the relationshis between organisms and their environment

ecosystem a system formed by the interaction of a group of organisms with their environment

endangered likely to become extinct

entomologist person who studies insects

environment the world around us

equatorial belt imaginary circle around the earth's surface, that divides the earth into the Northern Hemisphere and the Southern Hemisphere.

endemism something peculiar to a particular region

erosion wearing away by wind and rain

evolve the process by which something changes very slowly over a long time

extinct an animal or plant that no longer exists

genetics the study of inheritance

genus group with common attributes

habitat the place where a plant or animal lives

hemisphere the northern or southern half of the earth as divided by the equator

invertebrate animal without a backbone

larva/larvae immature form of an
   invertebrate e.g. a caterpillar

litter offspring produced by a mammal

marine biologist person who studies living
   things in seas and oceans

native a plant or animal that occurs in a
   place naturally

nomadic an animal with no fixed home

organism a single form of life, such as a
   plant, animal or fungus

pesticide chemical that kills invertebrates

plankton microscopic plants and animals
   that live in water

pollution substances released that harm
   the environment

pupa stage in an invertebrate life cycle where
   a larva changes into an adult

predator an animal that kills and eats
   other animals

rainforest dense forest in hot, wet equatorial
   areas

reintroduction the process of reintroducing
an animal or plant into an area from which
it has not been present for a while

satellite a machine launched into space to
orbit the Earth. From space it can send
back images of the Earth's surface which
can help conservationists assess conditions
in various regions.

species a type of animal or plant survey
assess something by sampling

survey gathering of a sample of data

sustainable can be maintained

threat risk or danger

transmitter An electronic device that sends
an electronic wave to another device

tropical something found in the tropics, a
region of the earth's surface characterised
by hot and wet climate

vertebrate animal with a backbone

vulnerable in conservation terms, a species
whose status is threatened by declining
numbers

zoologist person who studies animals

Copyright © ticktock Entertainment Ltd 2004
First published in Great Britain in 2004 by ticktock Media Ltd.,
Unit 2, Orchard Business Centre, North Farm Road, Tunbridge Wells, Kent, TN2 3XF
We would like to thank: Elizabeth Wiggans and Jenni Rainford for their help with this book.
ISBN 1 86007 591 6 HB   ISBN 1 86007 585 1 PB
Printed in China
A CIP catalogue record for this book is available from the British Library.

Picture Credits
Alamy: 1 & 6b, 7r, 15 all, 22 all. Frank Lane Picture Library: 2-3c, 23 all. Corbis: 6-7c, 10cl, 10b, 11t, 11c, 14cl, 14b, 16-17 all, 18b, 18-19t & b, 21b, 21r, 24, 25t, 28b, 29 all. IUCN: 8b, 9c. Natural History Museum: 4t. Science Photo Library: 4-5c, 5r, 9r, 19r, 20l, 21t, 26-27 all.

this is my faith

Sikhism

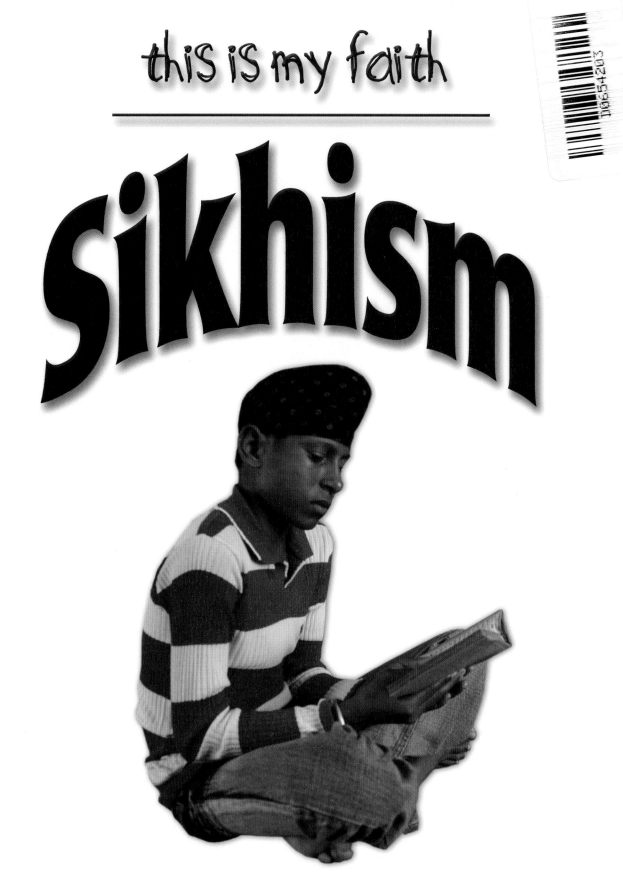

by David Dalton

ticktock

Copyright © ticktock Entertainment Ltd 2006
First published in Great Britain in 2006 by ticktock Media Ltd.,
Unit 2, Orchard Business Centre, North Farm Road,
Tunbridge Wells, Kent, TN2 3XF

We would like to thank: Jean Coppendale, Honor Head, Plan UK and Plan International,
and Kanwaljit Singh.

With special thanks to Inderjeet Singh and his family

ISBN 978 1 84696 031 4
Printed in China
3 4 5 6 7 8 9 10

Picture credits
t = top, b = bottom, c = centre, l = left, r = right,
OFC = outside front cover, OBC = outside back cover

Alamy: 7b, 9c, 9b, 11c, 13t, 13c, 14b, 17c, 19t, 21b, 23t, 27c. Art Directors and Trip Photo
Library: 12b, 13b, 27b. Corbis: 11b, 19b, 23c, 23b, 25t, 26, 28b. Plan UK and Plan
International: OFC, 1, 2, 4b, 5all, 6, 7t, 8, 12t, 16, 17b, 18, 20, 21t, 21c, 22t, 24t, 26t, OBC.
World Religions PL/ Christine Osborne: 7c, 9t, 11t, 15b, (Prem Kapoor: 15t, 29b) 17t, 19c, 22,
24b, 27t, 29t.

Every effort has been made to trace the copyright holders, and we apologize in advance for any
unintentional omissions. We would be pleased to insert the appropriate acknowledgements in any
subsequent edition of this publication.

Contents

Words that appear in **bold** are explained in the glossary.

I am a Sikh

"My name is Inderjeet Singh. I am 13 years old and I live in a small village in the Punjab, in India. I am a **Sikh**."

"The word 'Sikh' in the **Punjabi** language means 'disciple'. Sikhs are the **disciples** of God who follow the writings and teachings of the ten **Sikh Gurus**."

This is Inderjeet. Sikhism teaches him that all people are equal. This means that Sikhs treat men and women, and people of different faiths in the same way.

All Sikh men and boys wear a turban on their heads and have Singh as part of their name.

"Being a Sikh is important in every part of my life, in what I believe, how I behave, how I look and even my name."

"I say prayers every day. These are from the Guru's teachings. I also read from the Guru Granth Sahib, our special book, every day."

Reading the writings of the Gurus helps Inderjeet to learn about how he should live.

The special Khanda symbol is shown on the Sikh flag and is often used to decorate turbans.

"The **Khanda symbol** is very special to the Sikhs. It is the double-edged sword of life surrounded by the circle of **eternity**."

My family

"I live with my mother, two brothers and two sisters. My father is dead. We say he left us to be with God."

"My home is small. We have three little rooms which is enough for all of us."

Inderjeet's father was called Manjeet Singh. His mother's name is Amarjeet Kaur.

Inderjeet's mother and his sister have their own names and also the name Kaur.

"When girls are **confirmed** they are given the extra name Kaur, which means 'princess'. Boys are given the name Singh, which means 'lion'."

"Parents often help their children to learn about Sikhism by telling them stories of the Gurus. The stories teach us to be proud of our beliefs."

Children are taught the stories of the Gurus at home and at school.

A typical Sikh meal is a type of bread called roti and different vegetable curries. Men and women cook and share all household jobs.

"We help our mother around the house by doing the housework. Then we help her to prepare the family meals."

What I believe

"Sikhs try to follow the teachings of the Guru Granth Sahib. This is the work of our Sikh Gurus, or holy teachers, which teaches us how to live and behave."

"A holy man called Guru Nanak was told by God to teach people a new religion in which everyone was treated the same."

Inderjeet enjoys reading about the lives of the Gurus. The stories are a good example for him to follow and are very interesting.

Guru Nanak was born in 1469. His family believed in the Hindu religion but Guru Nanak chose to start a new religion called Sikhism.

"The first Sikh teacher was Guru Nanak. He taught that there is only one God and that everyone is equal."

"Guru Nanak travelled around telling people about Sikhism and teaching them to treat all people with kindness. An early follower was Bhai Lalo, a carpenter."

Nanak stayed in the simple home of Bhai Lalo. Nanak liked it better than the homes of the rich because Bhai (left) had earned his money honestly by hard work.

The Gurmukhi script was developed by Guru Angad so that he could write down Guru Nanak's teachings. Gurmukhi means 'the mouth of the Guru'.

"When Nanak died, Guru Angad became the leader of Sikhism. He improved the Gurmukhi script and collected the writings of Guru Nanak."

9

LEARN MORE: What is Sikhism?

- Sikhism began in 1499 in the Punjab, in north-west India. There are over 25 million Sikhs living in India today. Most Sikhs live in the Punjab region. Sikhism is the world's fifth most popular religion.

WORLD MAP

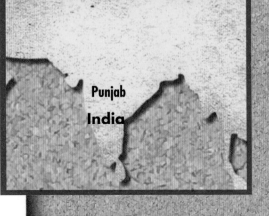

Britain

EUROPE

NORTH AMERICA

Malaysi
Singapore

Austra

Punjab
India

- There are now thousands of Sikhs in Britain, Europe, North America and Australia. There are also Sikhs living in many other parts of the world, such as Malaysia and Singapore.

One of the Panj Pyare pours **amrit** into the hands of Guru Gobind Singh as part of the confirmation. This is to show that the Guru is equal with the people that follow him, although he is a leader.

• Guru Gobind Singh founded the Khalsa which started with five men who said that they were willing to die for their faith. These men are known as the **Panj Pyare**, or 'the five beloved ones'. The Panj Pyare formed the first **Khalsa** with the Guru.

• Sikhs worship in a temple called a **gurdwara**. Most gurdwaras have a prayer hall where the holy book, the Guru Granth Sahib, is kept.

Each gurdwara has a **langar** hall. This is a room where everyone gathers after the gurdwara service to share a meal. Langar means 'shared food'.

The other Gurus

"Each of the Gurus gave us teachings to follow. Guru Arjun and Guru Teg Bahadur died for their faith."

"Some of the Gurus were forced to fight to protect **Hindus** and other Sikhs from the cruelty of rulers who wanted everyone to change their faith to **Islam**."

Har Krishan was known as the Child Guru. He was only five years old when he became a Guru. He died of **smallpox** when he was eight years old.

11

Guru Gobind Singh was a skilled horseman, archer and hunter. He is usually shown with a falcon, a hunting bird.

"I am really interested in Guru Gobind Singh who gave his life fighting for the Sikhs. He was very brave. I read about him in the books at school."

"Guru Ram Das built Amritsar which is the holy city of the Sikhs. He also wrote a hymn that is sung at Sikh weddings."

Amritsar was a forest before Guru Ram Das started to build the lake there which now surrounds the Golden Temple.

When the Golden Temple was finished, Guru Arjan Dev put the first copy of the Guru Granth Sahib inside the Temple.

"Guru Arjan Dev was the son of Guru Ram Das. He built the beautiful Golden Temple on the lake in Amritsar, in India."

LEARN MORE: A special book

- The Sikh holy book is called Guru Granth Sahib. It contains hymns and teachings written by the Gurus and other holy men.

- When the tenth Guru, Gobind Singh, died in 1708, he said that Sikhs did not need a living Guru, but that the Guru Granth Sahib should be their Guru.

The Guru Granth Sahib is written in a script called Gurmukhi.

These children are learning to read Gurmukhi in a gurdwara school.

- This symbol is known as **Ik Onkar**. It means 'there is only one God'. These are the first words of the Sikh holy book.

The Ik Onkar symbol is often used to decorate Sikh objects.

People who look after the Guru Granth Sahib and read it out loud in the gurdwara are known as **granthi**.

- The Guru Granth Sahib is kept on a raised place called a **manji** in the main hall of the gurdwara. It is kept there so that everyone can see it and read it.

- When it is not in use the Guru Granth Sahib may be covered by a cloth called a rumalla. Women as well as men can be a granthi, or reader.

The woman at the back of this picture is holding a fan called a chor. It is waved over the Guru Granth Sahib as a sign of respect.

The Five Ks

"Sikhs who are part of the Khalsa wear five symbols of their faith. These are called the **Five Ks** because each begins with the letter K in the Punjabi language."

"Kesh is the word for long, uncut hair and a beard. As Sikhs we do not cut our hair. We keep it tidy by tying it up in a turban or **patka**."

Inderjeet keeps his hair tied up in a patka. He wears a turban for special occasions.

The kangha is a wooden comb used by Sikhs to keep their hair tidy. It is a symbol of cleanliness.

"We comb our hair with a kangha. We also wear special cotton shorts called kacha which are comfortable to wear."

"The kirpan is a short sword. It is a symbol of the fight against evil and for truth."

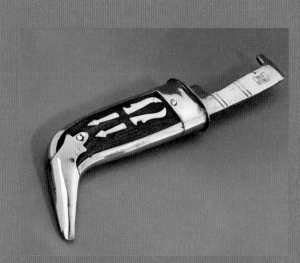

Today the kirpan is worn as a symbol to show that Sikhs are prepared to fight for the beliefs of the poor and weak.

This Sikh wears the kara and carries a kirpan across his shoulder.

"The kara is a steel bangle which Sikhs wear all the time. It reminds us to do the right things the Gurus taught us."

17

Why Sikhs wear turbans

"Sikh men never cut their hair or beard because this is what the Guru Gobind Singh asked. He said that we should wear a turban to keep our long hair tidy and safe."

"When we wear a turban we are showing our love for God and that we are happy to be Sikhs."

Inderjeet can tie the turban himself but his mother often helps him. It takes time and practise to do it well.

Very young boys and girls wear a piece of cloth, called a patka, tied around their hair until they are old enough to wear a turban.

"Turbans come in every colour and pattern. But the most commonly worn are white, deep blue and orange."

"There are many different ways to tie a turban. Men keep their hair inside by tying it into a top knot or making it into a plait."

Many Sikhs wear a patka under their turban.

Some Sikh women wear a turban and a scarf to keep their hair tidy and to stay cool in the hot weather.

"Most women just tie their hair back in a bun. They cover their hair with a scarf when they visit the gurdwara as a sign of respect."

Where I worship

"Sikhs can pray anywhere at any time but the place where a lot of Sikhs gather to pray is called a gurdwara, which means Guru's door."

"We take our shoes off and wash our hands and feet before we enter the gurdwara. This is to keep the gurdwara clean and as a sign of respect."

Sikhs put their hands together, bow their heads and close their eyes when they pray. This is so they can concentrate on the prayers and God.

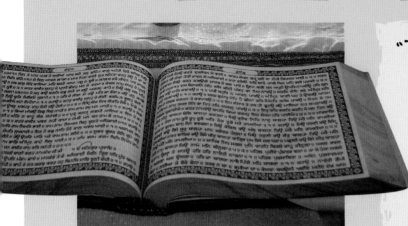

At the end of the service the Guru Granth Sahib is opened anywhere. The words on that page are read out, there is a blessing and the service is finished.

"There is a gurdwara at my school which I visit every day. There are services throughout the day. I go in and stay for as long as I can before lessons."

"Everyone sits cross-legged on the floor of the gurdwara. This is to show that we are all equal."

We make sure that we don't point our feet towards the Guru Granth Sahib.

Everyone gives something to the langar meal. They can bring food to cook, give money, or help to prepare and serve the meal.

"At the end of the service everyone goes to the langar hall to share a meal. People from all religions can join in the service and share the meal."

Special festivals

"One of our most important festivals is **Baisakhi**. This is the day that we remember when the Khalsa was created and when the Sikhs were given the Five Ks which have become our uniform."

"Baisakhi takes place in April and is also part of the harvest festival when we celebrate the gathering in of new crops."

During Baisakhi, langar food is served in the streets.

Traditional folk dances from the Punjab, called the Gidda and Bhangra, are performed during the Baisakhi celebrations.

"At Baisakhi we visit gurdwaras and listen to readings from the Guru Granth Sahib. Many people decorate their houses with flowers."

"Sikhs also celebrate Diwali. This is when we remember the release of Guru Hargobind from the Muslims. Lamps are lit outside the gurdwaras and we are given sweets."

The biggest Diwali celebration takes place at the Golden Temple in Amritsar, which is lit up with thousands of lights.

During Hola Mahalla the Sikhs give displays of horseriding and swordsmanship.

"Hola Mahalla is a festival when Sikhs show off their fighting skills. There is a parade and mock battles. Afterwards we have music and poetry competitions."

Gurpurb festivals

"We have many festivals when we remember times in the Gurus' lives. These festivals are called Gurpurbs and often there is a procession when the Guru Granth Sahib is carried through the streets for everyone to see."

"The most important Gurpurbs are the birthdays of Guru Nanak and Guru Gobind Singh and the deaths of Guru Arjan and Guru Teg Bahadur."

Gurpurb celebrations begin with a reading of the Guru Granth Sahib by a group of granthi. They read the Guru Granth Sahib non-stop, from beginning to end, which takes forty-eight hours.

These Sikhs are performing Gatka, a type of Sikh **martial art,** during a procession to celebrate Guru Nanak's birthday in India. The celebrations can last for up to three days.

"During the gurpurbs there are parades through the streets and special displays. Many gurdwaras are decorated with flags and flowers and some are lit up with candles and lights. We have a special service with hymns and prayers. After the prayers, Karah Parasaad is served. This is a sweet-tasting food which has been blessed."

Special occasions

"We have lots of special ceremonies to mark important times in our lives. In many families, when a boy reaches a certain age, he goes to the gurdwara and his first turban is tied on by the granthi."

"For me, the most important ceremony was my confirmation, or amrit, when I became a Khalsa."

During the amrit ceremony, the person drinks the amrit, or holy nectar, five times and has some sprinkled on his hair and eyes.

The amrit is stirred by Sikhs who are acting out the parts of the Panj Pyare.

"For the confirmation ceremony, the amrit is prepared. A bowl is filled with water, and sugar is added while prayers are said."

"During a wedding ceremony the groom wears a scarf called a palla. The bride holds one end and the bridegroom holds the other end to show their **unity.**"

At the ceremony the couple sits in front of the Guru Granth Sahib and the granthi explains the duties of married life.

Friends and family sing hymns around the coffin before the body is taken to be cremated.

"When someone dies we believe that their soul leaves their body. The body is usually **cremated** and the ashes are put into the river."

LEARN MORE: Holy places

- Sikhs visit historical places to remind themselves of important events in the lives of the Sikh gurus.

- One of the most important places for Sikhs is the Hari Mandir, or Golden Temple, in the city of Amritsar in Punjab, north-west India. Thousands of people visit the temple every day.

The Hari Mandir or Golden Temple in Amritsar. The name Hari Mandir means means 'eternal throne'.

The house where Guru Nanak was born. On one side of the house there is now a gurdwara called 'Nankana Sahib'.

- Guru Nanak, the founder of Sikhism, was born in the western Punjab, 75 kilometres from Lahore, Pakistan.

Guru Gobind Singh lived in Anandpur, in India, for nearly 25 years and the Anandpur Sahib gurdwara attracts thousands of visitors.

- The Anandpur Sahib gurdwara was built on the place where Guru Govind Singh gave amrit to the first five Sikhs and started the Khalsa. Anandpur is also known as the Holy City of Bliss.

Glossary

Ik Onkar

Amrit Sweetened holy water, used during the confirmation ceremony.

Baisakhi A festival to celebrate the creation of the Khalsa. It is sometimes spelled Vaiskahi.

Confirmation A ceremony which means that a Sikh is now a full member of the Sikh faith.

Cremated When a dead person's body is burned.

Disciples People who follow the teachings of a leader.

Diwali The Hindu festival of lights, also celebrated by Sikhs. Also spelled Divali.

Eternity Lasting for ever and ever, never ending.

Five Ks All Sikhs have to wear five items, known as the Five Ks (because they all begin with the letter 'k'), at all times. Kesh – long hair; kangha – a comb; kacha – cotton shorts; kirpan – a short sword; kara – a steel bangle.

Granthi Someone who looks after the Guru Granth Sahib and reads it out in the gurdwara.

Gurdwara This word means 'Guru's door'. A gurdwara is where Sikhs worship and is also the place where the Guru Granth Sahib is kept.

Gurmukhi Script This is a type of writing used for the Guru Granth Sahib. It was composed by Guru Angad.

Guru This word means 'teacher'. For Sikhs, the word means the first ten leaders of their faith.

Guru Granth Sahib The holy book of the Sikhs. 'Granth' is Punjabi for book and 'Sahib' means master in the Hindu language.

Hindu People who follow Hinduism, the ancient religion of India. Sikhism has some ideas that are similar to Hinduism.

30

Khanda symbol

A kangha (comb) and kara (a steel bangle) – two of the Five Ks

Hola Mahalla

This festival was first started by Guru Gobind Singh as a day for Sikhs to practise their fighting skills and to hold mock battles.

Ik Onkar This means 'there is only one God.' These are the first words of the Guru Granth Sahib.

Islam The religion based on the teachings of the Prophet Mohammad. Its followers are called Muslims.

Khalsa People who have been confirmed as full members of the Sikh religion, and who wear the Five Ks.

Khanda Symbol This is sign that has a special meaning for Sikhs and which appears on all Sikh flags. It is made up of four weapons used by Sikhs at the time of Guru Govind Singh.

Langar A shared vegetarian meal, which is prepared after every Sikh service by volunteers.

Manji The 'throne' or special place for the Guru Granth Sahib in the gurdwara.

Martial art A way of defending yourself if you are attacked.

Panj Pyare This means 'the five beloved ones'. These are the five men who joined the first Khalsa with Guru Gobind Singh in 1699.

Patka The cloth young Sikh boys wear to cover their hair.

Punjabi The language spoken in the Punjab in India.

Sikh The word Sikh means 'a learner or disciple'. A Sikh is a believer in Sikhism, the religion founded by Guru Nanak in 1499.

Smallpox A disease which killed many people in the past. It is quite rare today.

Unity Being joined together as one.

Index